Presented to:

_____

From:

_____

Date:

_____

Jesus Calling®
The Story of Easter

Sarah Young

Illustrated by Katya Longhi

An Imprint of Thomas Nelson

Jesus Calling: The Story of Easter

© 2020 by Sarah Young

Published in Nashville, Tennessee, by Tommy Nelson. Tommy Nelson is an imprint of Thomas Nelson. Thomas Nelson is a registered trademark of HarperCollins Christian Publishing, Inc.

A special thanks to Tama Fortner for her extensive work in shaping this manuscript. Illustrated by Katya Longhi.

Tommy Nelson titles may be purchased in bulk for educational, business, fund-raising, or sales promotional use. For information, please email SpecialMarkets@ThomasNelson.com.

Library of Congress Control Number: 2019013071

ISBN 978-1-4002-1032-9

Printed in China

20 21 22 23 24   LEO   10 9 8 7 6 5 4 3 2 1

Mfr: LEO / Heshan, China / January 2020 / PO #9563305

I dedicate this book to our grandchildren:
Elie, John, Caleb, Esther Grace, Joel, and Lawrence.
May you—and all who read this book—know
Jesus as your Savior and Friend.

Just as we have borne the likeness of the earthly man,
so shall we bear the likeness of the man from heaven.

—*1 Corinthians 15:49* NIV

Dear Parents and Grandparents,

So often, Easter rushes by with a flurry of bunnies, baskets, and bows. It's all too easy to allow the true meaning behind the celebration to slip away. Yet it's so important to teach our little ones—and to remind ourselves of—the truths behind the holiday.

God created us in His own image to love Him, to serve Him, and to live forever with Him. But even before He created the first man and woman, God knew that sin would come into the world and separate us from Him. So before the first star twinkled in the sky, God planned to send His Son to save His people.

And then, at the perfect time, Jesus did come. The Son of God, who never sinned, died to take the punishment for our sins. Three days later, He conquered death and rose from the grave.

One day, we will be raised up to a new and eternal life in a new and perfected body. Our hearts will be made like His—full of love and joy and peace. And we will spend forever with Him. That has always been God's plan. We need only to follow it.

I pray that this book will help you teach the children in your life about the true meaning of Easter and all that it promises.

I wish you and your family a meaningful and joy-filled Easter!

Sarah Young

That was his plan from before the beginning
of time—to show us his grace through Christ Jesus.
—2 Timothy 1:9 NLT

In the beginning, before anything was created, there was God.

And God had a beautiful plan.

He hung stars in the sky and set the earth in its place. Flowers bloomed, fish splashed, and birds soared. Animals of every kind crawled and ran and hopped. And He made people too.

God gave His creation everything it needed. And when His people needed someone to save them, He would send Jesus, His very own Son.

That was the beginning of Easter.

Jesus Calling

I created you. I created this world and everything in it. It is not possible for you to have a need that I cannot meet.

You created my inmost being; you knit me together in my mother's womb. I praise you because I am fearfully and wonderfully made.

—Psalm 139:13–14 NIV

God created the earth and everything in it.

His last creation—people—was His very best. First He took dust from the ground, shaped a man, and breathed life into him. God called him Adam. Then God made Eve, Adam's wife. They lived in a beautiful garden with God . . . until they broke God's only rule.

That was the beginning of sin. One day, every person would die. Their bodies would become dust again, but their souls would live on forever. And that's why Jesus would come—to save us from our sins so that we could live forever with Him.

Jesus Calling

I created a beautiful, perfect world for you. Then sin came into the world, and it brought trouble and sadness. But I have overcome the world. So stay close to Me.

Be kind to each other, tenderhearted,
forgiving one another, just as God
through Christ has forgiven you.
—Ephesians 4:32 NLT

All through the years, God watched over His people—even when times were hard.

Joseph knew all about tough times. His brothers hated him and sold him as a slave to Egypt. But God was with Joseph and helped him. Years later, when Joseph was rich and powerful, his brothers came to him for help.

Joseph had the power to punish them for what they had done to him. But he chose to forgive them instead, just as God chooses to forgive those who love and trust in Him.

Jesus Calling

When others treat you badly, you
have a chance to show them My grace.
Remember, I freely forgive all your sins.
Forgive them just as I forgive you.

"Jonah was in the stomach of the big fish for three days and three nights. In the same way, the Son of Man will be in the grave three days and three nights."
—Matthew 12:40 ICB

Jesus Calling

Let Me guide you. I have great plans for you, and I will be with you every step of the way!

God sent prophets to tell His people to obey Him and that Jesus was coming. One of those prophets was Jonah.

"Go to Nineveh," God said.

Jonah didn't like the people of Nineveh, so he tried to run away. Instead, a giant fish swallowed him! Jonah prayed and prayed. After three days, God made the fish spit Jonah out. So Jonah went to Nineveh and told the people about God, and they asked God for forgiveness for doing wrong.

Years later, God would raise Jesus from the grave after three days. And just like Jonah, Jesus' followers would spread the word about God's forgiveness—a message for *all* people.

When the time arrived that was set
by God the Father, God sent his Son.
—*Galatians 4:4* MSG

Jesus Calling

I am all-powerful. All of heaven and earth
is at My command. And yet . . . I gave
up the glory and perfection of heaven
to come to earth as a baby—for you.

When the time was just right, God sent His Son to be born as a baby in Bethlehem.

Jesus lived and learned and grew, just like you. But He never sinned—not even once! Jesus lived the perfect life so that those who believe in Him can be forgiven. Jesus taught that the most important thing is to love God more than anything else and to love others and treat them the way we would want to be treated.

Jesus answered, "Destroy this temple, and
I will build it again in three days." . . . But the
temple Jesus meant was his own body.

—John 2:19, 21 ICB

Jesus showed people how to live and love, how to help and forgive. Jesus talked about the prophets and all they had said about Him many years before He was born. He told people that He had come to take the punishment and die for their sins and that, after three days, He would be raised to life again.

Even though they didn't understand, many people loved Jesus and followed Him.

Jesus Calling
Someday I will take you into heaven—
to live with Me there forever.
But for now, just follow Me.

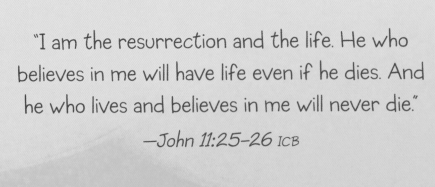

"I am the resurrection and the life. He who believes in me will have life even if he dies. And he who lives and believes in me will never die."

—John 11:25–26 ICB

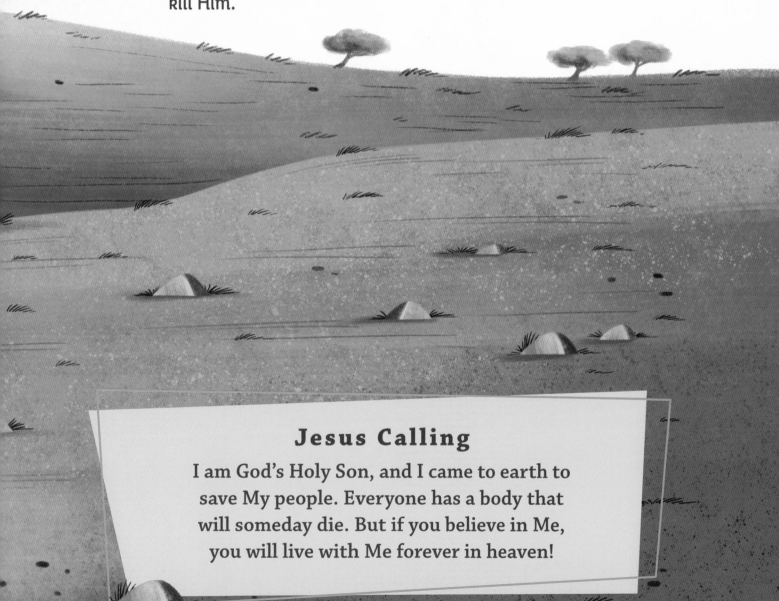

Jesus' friend Lazarus became so sick that he died. His body was buried in a tomb.

Four days later, Jesus came. He saw how sad His friends were and cried with them.

"Lazarus, come out!" Jesus called. And Lazarus did—because God has the power to raise the dead back to life again. Jesus is stronger than death.

The people were amazed! But not everyone was happy. Many of the religious leaders didn't like Jesus and planned to kill Him.

Jesus Calling

I am God's Holy Son, and I came to earth to save My people. Everyone has a body that will someday die. But if you believe in Me, you will live with Me forever in heaven!

He was wounded for the wrong things we did. . . .
The punishment, which made us well, was given to
him. And we are healed because of his wounds.

—Isaiah 53:5 ICB

Jesus ate one last supper with His friends. Then He went
to a garden to pray. The priests and Pharisees found Him
there. They arrested Jesus as His friends ran and left Him
alone.

Jesus was beaten and spit on and nailed to a cross. He
was punished for every kind of sin ever done.

Jesus' body was placed in a tomb. But that tomb wasn't
the end—it was why Jesus came! To give us a new beginning!

Jesus Calling

I poured out My Life on the cross so that I could
give you forgiveness and a home in heaven.
Trust Me as your Savior, Lord, and Friend.

He isn't here! He is risen from the
dead, just as he said would happen.

—Matthew 28:6 NLT

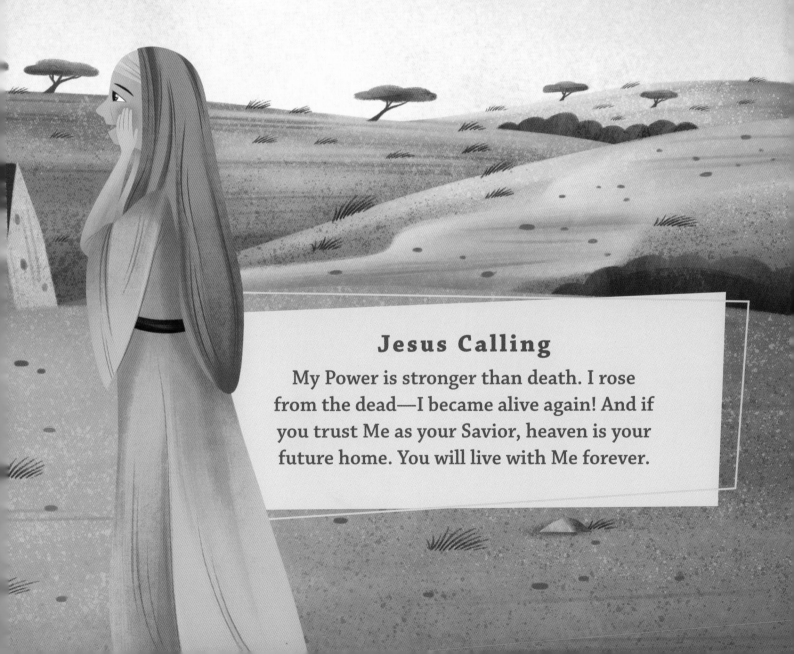

For three long days, Jesus' body lay in the tomb. His friends were scared and sad. They didn't understand why Jesus had died.

On Sunday morning, some women went to where Jesus was buried. But when they arrived, they found the tomb empty. Then the angel told them that Jesus was alive!

Jesus' body wasn't in the grave! He had risen from the dead on the third day, just as He promised He would.

Jesus Calling

My Power is stronger than death. I rose from the dead—I became alive again! And if you trust Me as your Savior, heaven is your future home. You will live with Me forever.

"Do you love me?"
"Yes, Lord," Peter said, "you know I love you."
"Then take care of my sheep," Jesus said.

—John 21:16 NLT

Some of Jesus' friends were fishing when they saw a man on the shore.

"Throw out your nets," the Man said.

Even though they had caught nothing all night, they threw their nets. And they caught more fish than the boat could hold!

"It's Jesus!" John cried to Peter. Then Peter jumped in the water and swam toward Jesus.

When Jesus had been arrested, Peter said he didn't even know Him—three times! Now when Jesus asked Peter if he loved Him, Peter said yes—three times.

"Feed my sheep," Jesus said. "Follow Me!" Jesus wanted Peter to take care of the people who believed in Him.

Jesus Calling

Bring your sins to Me. I already know all about them, and I'm just waiting to forgive you. Don't live in the darkness of sin. Live in the Light of My forgiveness.

God has said, "I will never leave
you; I will never abandon you."
—Hebrews 13:5 ICB

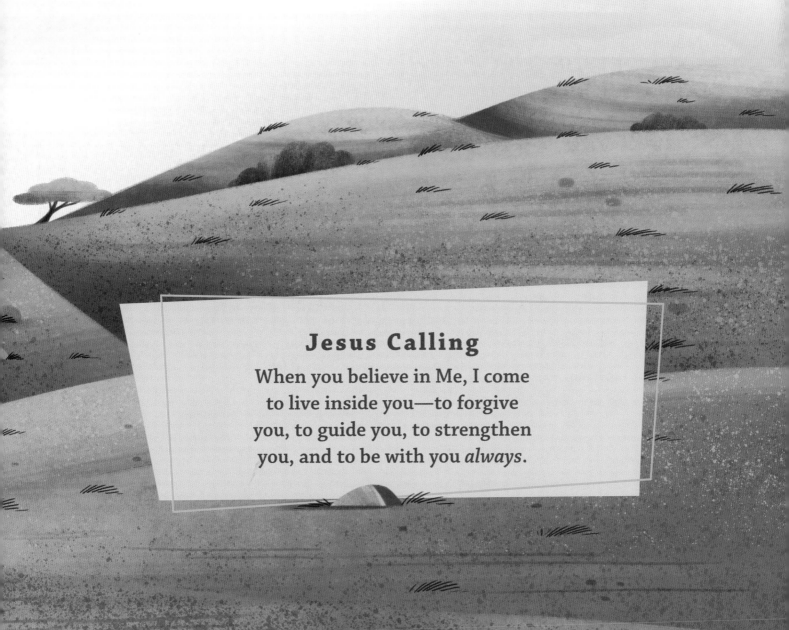

After Jesus came back to life, He walked on earth and talked and even ate with His friends. Then it was time to go back to heaven.

Jesus told His friends to teach the world why He came: to give us God's great love and to die on a cross to take away the sins of everyone who believes in Him.

Jesus promised His people a wonderful gift. The Holy Spirit of God would live inside them—and never, ever leave them.

Jesus Calling

When you believe in Me, I come to live inside you—to forgive you, to guide you, to strengthen you, and to be with you *always*.

God made a promise to us. And we are
waiting for what he promised—a new heaven
and a new earth where goodness lives.

—2 Peter 3:13 ICB

One day, Jesus will come back to earth again. And everyone in every country who loves and believes in Jesus will have a whole new life with Him! Our bodies will be made brand-new—they'll never know sickness or sadness or sin. Our hearts will be made to look like His, full of love and joy and peace.

Everything will be wonderful again—because Easter has always been God's beautiful plan, even before the world began.

Jesus Calling

Remember how much I love you. Remember that I made you just the way I want you to be. And remember that I died so you could live with Me forever. You are precious to Me!

"Look, I will make new heavens and a new earth. . . . My people will be happy forever because of the things I will make."

—Isaiah 65:17–18 ICB

My Dear Child,

I am your Lord, your God, your Savior, and your Friend. I created you in My image—to love as I love and to live close to Me.

I know you will make mistakes. Sometimes you will do the wrong thing, but I am always ready to forgive you. That's why I came into the world—to save you from your sins.

On that first Easter morning, when I rose up out of the tomb, I gave you a promise: One day, you will live with Me forever. There will be no more tears or sickness or sadness. Only love, joy, and peace.

Everything I did was to save you. That was My plan from the very beginning. So trust Me. Love Me. Follow Me. Pray and ask Me to help you. And remember, I will be with you always—taking care of you.

God showed how much he loved
us by sending his one and only
Son into the world so that we might
have eternal life through him.

—1 John 4:9 NLT